KB276134

Do As I Tell You!

Happy House

About Wise & Wide

- A systematic 6-level English reading program based on Lexile® measures
- Diverse and interesting topics chosen from the elementary curriculums of Korea and English speaking western countries
- Well-written books in various forms including fiction stories, descriptive texts, and classics retold
- The informative but original fiction stories grab your interest, leading to the easy and clear understanding of the educational content.
- Improve thinking skills with solid after-reading activities at all levels of the series.

Wise & Wide is a 6-level English reading program that consists of 60 books and each level is systematically divided by Lexile® measures. The Lexile® Framework for Reading is the most popular reading measuring system in American formal education curriculums and many English programs. Over 20 out of 50 states in the U.S. mark Lexile® measures directly on students' final report cards and over 300 well-known publishers adopt and use Lexile® measures.

Experience many kinds of readings written by professional writers from the U.S. and England. They used interesting topics that were carefully chosen after analyzing elementary curriculums from around the world including Korea, the U.S., England, and Australia among many others. Comprehensive after-reading activities including graphic organizers, speaking tasks, and After-reading Tests are ready for you.

Levels in the series and their corresponding Lexile® measures

Level	Lexile® measures	U.S. Grade
Level 1	Below 200L	Pre K - K
Level 2	190L - 400L	Lower Grade 1
Level 3	350L - 530L	Upper Grade 1
Level 4	420L - 650L	Grade 2
Level 5	520L - 940L	Grade 3 - 4
Level 6	830L - 1070L	Grade 5 - 6

* Smart Readers: Wise & Wide level 1 is applicable to the preschool level in the U.S.

* The source of the relationship between Lexile® measures and U.S. school grades: CCSS(Common Core State Standards) FOR ENGLISH LANGUAGE ARTS, APPENDIX A (2012, which is used by 45 states in the U.S.)

Topic List

	Level 1	Level 2	Level 3	Level 4	Level 5	Level 6
Book 1	Science>Biology: The hibernation of animals Story	Science>Biology: Living and nonliving things Story	Science>Biology> Animals & the Environment: Sea otters Story	Environment> Living with nature: The diver & the persimmon tree Story	Science>Biology> Animal: Amazing animals of the Amazon Story	Science>Biology: Germs, transmitted diseases Story
Book 2	Literature> World classics: Aesop's fables Story	Literature> Traditional fairy tale: Old tales about stones Story	Social Studies> Economy: To run a business to make and save money Story	Science>Biology> Plants: Photosynthesis Story	Science>Earth science: Earth's layers, earthquakes, volcanoes, and earth's atmosphere Report	Mathematics> Sequence: The golden ratio & the Fibonacci sequence Story
Book 3	Science>Physics: How shadows are formed Story	Literature> World classics: Peter Pan Story	Science>Scientific technology: Nanobots Story	Literature>Myths: World's creation stories Story	Literature> Legend: The story of King Arthur Story	Literature>Myths: Constellation myths Story
Book 4	Literature> Traditional literature: The Talmud Story	Science>Biology> Animal: Polar bears Story	Science>Biology> Animal: Mountain gorillas Story	Social Studies> Cultural anthropology: Amazing ancient cultures of the world Story	Science> Earth science: Clouds and weather Story	Literature> Human & animals: The friendship between a girl and a horse Story
Book 5	Social Studies> Ethics: Rules in daily life Story	Science>Biology: The five senses Report	Social Studies> Cultural anthropology: Astonishing festivals Report	Art>Music: Stories from two operas Story	Social Studies> World culture & history: The Renaissance Story	Sports> Board sports: Surfing & snowboarding Story
Book 6	Social Studies> World geography & travel: Tourist attractions around the world Story	Science>Biology> Animal: Dinosaurs Story	Science> Astronomy: The solar system Story	Social Studies> People: Three great people who overcame hardships Story	Science>Scientific technology: The wonderful world of robots Report	Art>Music: Composers of the Romantic Era Report
Book 7	Science> Space science: The life of astronauts Report	Social Studies> Cultural anthropology: Mythological monsters from around the world Report	Mathematics> Elementary mathematics: Numbers, measurement, shapes and data Report	Science & Social Studies> Technology & culture: Inventions from around the world Report	Art>Works of art: Famous paintings Report	Social Studies> Human & animals: Animals in action for human Report
Book 8	Social Studies> Cultural anthropology: Various living cultures of the world Story	Art>Music: Instruments in the orchestra Story	Social Studies> Life safety: Learning and using outdoor survival skills Story	Social Studies> History: The California Gold Rush Report	Social Studies & Science> Psychology: Psychology in everyday life Story	Literature> World classics: The Merchant of Venice Story
Book 9	Social Studies> Jobs: Interviews about jobs Report	Science>Scientific technology: Developments in technology in different times Story	Social Studies> Politics>Election: Running for 3rd grade class president Story	Literature> World classics: Stories of Sherlock Holmes Story	Literature> World classics: Adrift in the Pacific Story	Social Studies> History & People: Great world leaders in history Report
Book 10	Literature>Traditional fairy tale: Eastern and Western folk tales on the same theme Story	Sports>Winter sports: Various aspects of some Winter Olympic sports Report	Literature> World classics: Short stories by O. Henry Story	Sports> Ball games: Various aspects of popular ball games Report	Social Studies> History: Famous events that changed world history Report	Art & Social Studies> Art: Stories about the creation, distribution, and preservation of paintings Report

How to Use This Book

•Before Reading

You can easily find the topic and what kind of story you are about to read.

•The text

All the stories were written by professional writers from the U.S. and England, so you will read authentic and appropriate English sentences and expressions in every book in the series.

•Pop Quiz

Check out right away if you understand what you have just read by solving a pop quiz that checks your comprehension.

•Key Words

The key words and expressions on each page are listed for you to easily study them.

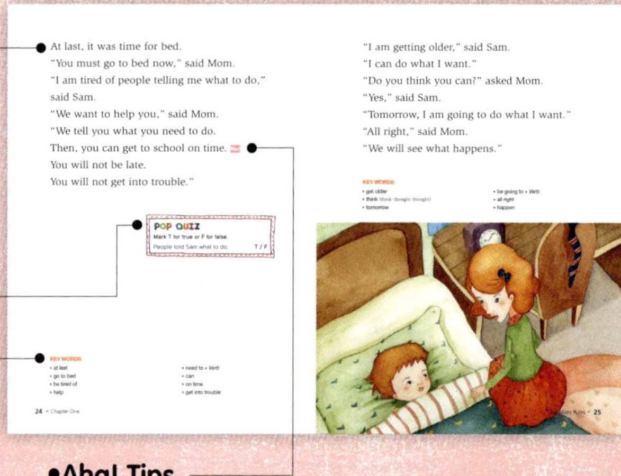

•Aha! Tips

Download free Korean explanations at *www.ihappyhouse.co.kr* for all of the sentences marked with "Aha!". These explain cultural, scientific, and economic knowledge or they deal with aspects of English such as grammatical structures or idiomatic expressions. There are lots of "Aha! Tips" to help you understand the text.

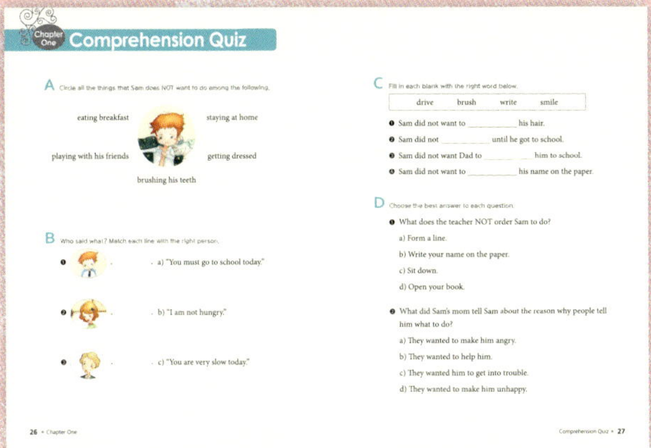

•Comprehension Quiz

After reading one chapter, solve various questions to find out if you fully understand the content.

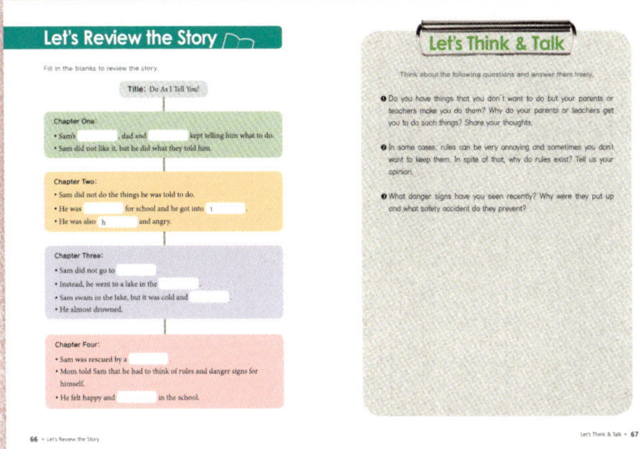

•Let's Review the Story /
•Let's Think & Talk

Fill in the blanks in the organizer to summarize the whole story. Express your own thinking and feelings about the story by answering the questions. You can build up logic and reasoning skills for your essay examinations in the future.

Appendix

Audio CD

In the CD audio book form, the texts are read vividly by American professional voice actors.

After-reading Test

Solve an additionally provided After-reading Test for each book.

The Korean translation, Answer Keys, a Word Quiz, a Word List, and Aha! Tips for each book

You can download them for free at *www.ihappyhouse.co.kr*

Before Reading

Do As I Tell You!

Level 1–5,
Lexile® 150L

•Social Studies〉Ethics
•Story

Why do rules exist?

You have probably been told to 'Cross at a green light', 'Don't step on the grass', etc. You have probably been told to follow these rules. A rule is a kind of law that everyone decides to follow. The rules above help maintain public order. Rules, however, are needed not only in public places but also in everyday life. Getting up early, having breakfast on time, being neatly dressed, not being late for school, etc. are important rules for life.

Do you follow these different kinds of rules well? Perhaps you follow the rules for public order well, but are annoyed by your parents' rules for everyday life. Let's find out why rules should be kept through Sam's story in the book.

Summary

Sam is angry at his mom, dad and teacher who don't let him do as he wants and make him do this and do that. At home in the morning, his mom tells him to get up quickly, get dressed, and get ready for school. But Sam wants to sleep in! Then Dad tells him to get in his car. But Sam wants to walk to school. Why can't he do what he wants? At school, his teacher tells him to sit quietly and solve a quiz. But Sam wants to move around the classroom and play in the school yard. Who made such annoying rules and why did he or she make them? Tomorrow for one day, Sam decides not to listen to what adults say, but to do as he pleases! Will Sam be able to have a fun and joyful day?

Contents

Do As I Tell You!

2   About Wise & Wide
4   How to Use This Book
6   Before Reading

Chapter One
10   Too Many Rules
26   Comprehension Quiz

Chapter Two
28   I Will Do What I Want
40   Comprehension Quiz

Chapter Three
42   Deep Water
52   Comprehension Quiz

Chapter Four
54   Happy and Safe
64   Comprehension Quiz

66   Let's Review the Story

67   Let's Think & Talk

68   Let's Review the Story (Answers)

71   After-reading Test

Do As I Tell You!

Too Many Rules

Sam was asleep.

"Sam!" said Mom.

"It is time to wake up."

Sam groaned.

He did not want to wake up.

He wanted to stay in bed.

"You must get up," said Mom. **Aha!**

"You must go to school today."

Sam did not want to go to school.

He wanted to stay at home.

"Come on," said Mom.

"Get up now."

KEY WORDS

- too
- rule
- asleep
- it is (for + *Noun*) time to + *Verb*
- wake up (wake-woke-woken)
- groan
- stay
- must + *Verb*
- get up (get-got-gotten)
- go to school (go-went-gone)
- Come on!
- now

"I do not want to get up," said Sam.

"Do as I tell you," said Mom. 

She went away.

Sam sat up.

He was tired, so he lay down again.

Mom came again.

"Sam!" called Mom.

"Are you up yet?"

Sam got out of bed.

"Yes, I am," he called.

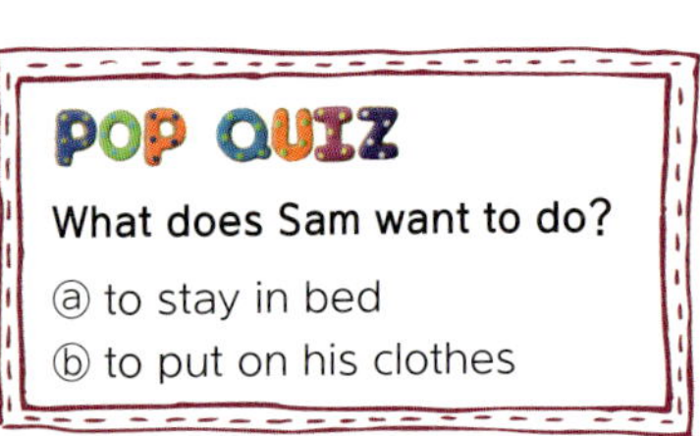

"You must get dressed," said Mom.

"I do not want to get dressed," said Sam.

"Do as I tell you," said Mom.

Sam did not want to get dressed.

But he put on his clothes.

- **do** (do-did-done)
- **tell** (tell-told-told)
- **go away**
- **sit up** (sit-sat-sat)
- **tired**
- **so**
- **lie down** (lie-lay-lain)
- **again**
- **call**
- **up**
- **yet**
- **get out of**
- **get dressed**
- **put on** (put-put-put)
- **clothes**

"Sam!" called Mom.
"Come and eat
breakfast." 
Sam did not want
to eat breakfast.
He was not hungry.
"Come on," said
Mom.
"You must eat it."
"I do not want to eat it," said Sam.
"I am not hungry."

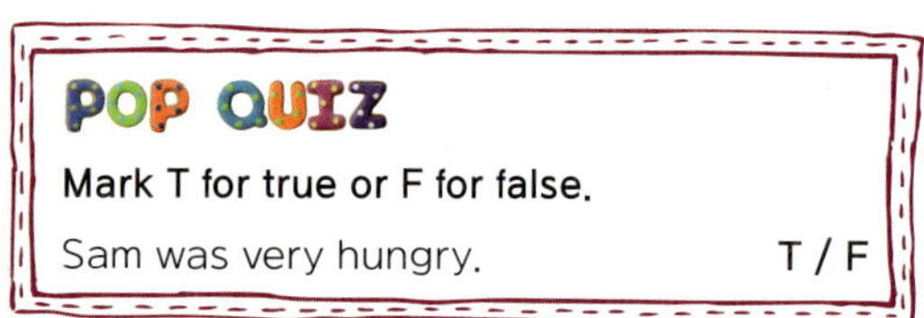

KEY WORDS

- **eat** (eat-ate-eaten)   - **breakfast**   - hungry

"Do as I tell you," said Mom.

Sam ate his breakfast.

He ate it slowly.

"Hurry," said Mom.

"You will be late for school."

Sam ate all his breakfast.

"I am ready to go to school now," he said.

- slowly
- hurry
- be late for

- all
- be ready to + *Verb*

"No, you are not," said Mom.

"First, you must brush your teeth."

"I do not want to brush my teeth," said Sam.

"Do as I tell you," said Mom.

Sam went to the bathroom.

He brushed his teeth.

But he began to feel angry.

"There are too many rules," he said.

"Everyone keeps telling me what to do."

"Now you must brush your hair," said Mom.

"I do not want to brush my hair," said Sam.

"Do as I tell you," said Mom.

Sam sighed.

But he brushed his hair.

KEY WORDS

- first
- brush
- teeth
- bathroom
- begin (begin-began-begun)
- feel (feel-felt-felt)

- angry
- everyone
- keep + *Verb*-ing (keep-kept-kept)
- hair
- sigh

"Sam!" called Dad.

"You are very slow today.

I will drive you to school.

Then, you will not be late.

Get in the car."

"I do not want to go in the car," said Sam.

KEY WORDS

- **drive** (drive-drove-driven)
- **then**
- **late**
- **get in**
- **go in the car**
- **run after** (run-ran-run)
- **forget** (forget-forgot-forgotten)
- **get**
- **when**
- **smile**
- **until**
- **get to**

"Do as I tell you," said Dad.

Sam got in the car.

Mom ran after him.

"You have forgotten your bag!" she called.

"Go and get your bag," said Dad.

"I do not want to get my bag," said Sam.

"Do as you are told," said Dad.

Sam was angry.

He did not like it when Mom and Dad told
him what to do.

He did not smile until he got to school.

When Sam got to school, he saw his friends.

He went to play with them.

"Form a line," said the teacher.

"It is time for school to begin.

We must go inside."

Sam did not want to go into the classroom.

He wanted to stay outside.

He wanted to play with his friends.

They went into the classroom.

"Sit down," said the teacher.

Sam did not want to sit down.

He wanted to walk around.

He wanted to jump and run.

"Do as I tell you," said the teacher.

It was time for a quiz.

"Write your name on the paper," said the teacher.

Sam did not want to write his name.

He did not want to do the quiz.

"Do as I tell you," said the teacher.

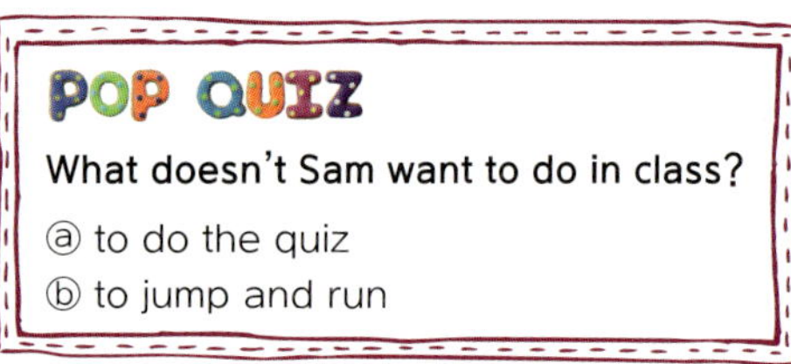

KEY WORDS

- sit down
- walk around (*cf.* walk)
- jump
- it is time for + *Noun*
- quiz

- write (write-wrote-written)
- paper
- day
- go on

The day went on.

The teachers told Sam what to do.

Mom and Dad told him what to do.

At last, it was time for bed.

"You must go to bed now," said Mom.

"I am tired of people telling me what to do,"
said Sam.

"We want to help you," said Mom.

"We tell you what you need to do.

Then, you can get to school on time. 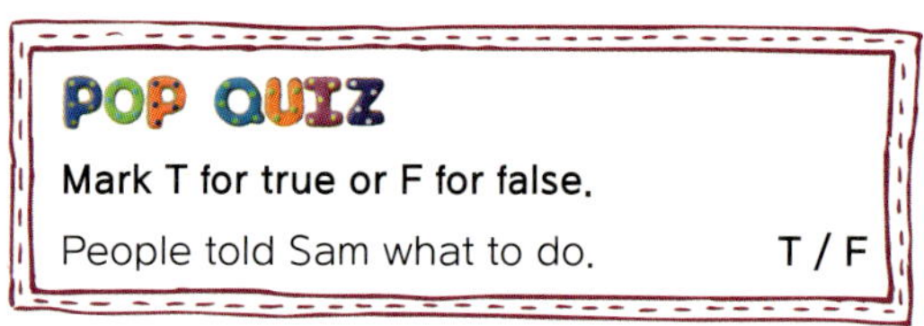

You will not be late.

You will not get into trouble."

KEY WORDS

- at last
- go to bed
- be tired of
- help

- need to + *Verb*
- can
- on time
- get into trouble

"I am getting older," said Sam.

"I can do what I want."

"Do you think you can?" asked Mom.

"Yes," said Sam.

"Tomorrow, I am going to do what I want."

"All right," said Mom.

"We will see what happens."

KEY WORDS

- get older
- **think** (think-thought-thought)
- tomorrow
- be going to + *Verb*
- all right
- happen

Comprehension Quiz

A Circle all the things that Sam does NOT want to do among the following.

eating breakfast

staying at home

playing with his friends

getting dressed

brushing his teeth

B Who said what? Match each line with the right person.

❶ •

• a) "You must go to school today."

❷ •

• b) "I am not hungry."

❸ •

• c) "You are very slow today."

C Fill in each blank with the right word below.

| drive | brush | write | smile |

❶ Sam did not want to _____________ his hair.

❷ Sam did not _____________ until he got to school.

❸ Sam did not want Dad to _____________ him to school.

❹ Sam did not want to _____________ his name on the paper.

D Choose the best answer to each question.

❶ What does the teacher NOT order Sam to do?

a) Form a line.

b) Write your name on the paper.

c) Sit down.

d) Open your book.

❷ What did Sam's mom tell Sam about the reason why people tell him what to do?

a) They wanted to make him angry.

b) They wanted to help him.

c) They wanted him to get into trouble.

d) They wanted to make him unhappy.

I Will Do What I Want

The next morning, Sam woke up late.

"What time is it?" he said to himself.

He looked at the clock.

It was nearly time for school!

He jumped out of bed.

He pulled on his clothes.

"Why didn't you wake me?" he said to Mom.

"You can do what you want today," said Mom.

"Good," said Sam.

"I do not want any breakfast.

I am not hungry."

"All right," said Mom.

"You might be hungry later."

"I do not care," said Sam.

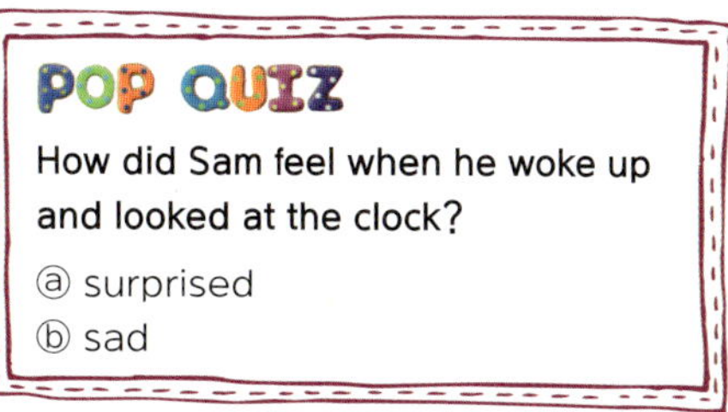

KEY WORDS

- What time is it?
- say to oneself (say-said-said)
- look at
- clock
- nearly
- jump out of
- pull on
- any
- might + *Verb*
- later
- care

"I am not going to brush my teeth," said Sam.

"All right," said Mom.

"Your breath might smell bad.

Your teeth might go bad."

Sam did not believe Mom.

"I do not care," he said.

"I am not going to brush my hair either."

"All right," said Mom.

"You might look untidy."

"I do not care," said Sam.

"Hurry up!" called Dad.
"You will be late for school.
I will drive you there."
"No, thank you," said Sam. Aha!
"I will walk to school today."
"But you will be late," said Dad.
"I do not care," said Sam.
He walked down the street.

Mom ran after him.

"You have forgotten your bag!" she called.

"I do not need my bag," said Sam.

"I will go without it."

So Sam walked to school.

He did not go in the car.

He did not take his bag.

He did not brush his hair.

He did not brush his teeth.

He did not eat any breakfast.

"This is good," he said.

"I can do what I want.

Nobody will tell me what to do."

KEY WORDS

- without
- take (take-took-taken)

- nobody

When Sam got to school, the yard was empty.

Everyone was inside.

He walked into the classroom.

"Where have you been?" asked the teacher.

"You are very late."

The teacher was angry.

"I am sorry," said Sam.

"All right," said the teacher. **Aha!**

KEY WORDS

- **yard**
- **empty** (↔ full)
- **bring** (bring-brought-brought)
- **learn** (↔ teach)
- **anything**

"Where is your bag?"

"I did not bring my bag," said Sam.

"Where are your books?" asked the teacher.

"They are at home," said Sam.

"Then how will you learn anything today?"
asked the teacher.

The teacher was very angry indeed.

She sent Sam to the principal.

The principal was angry with Sam, too.

Sam had to pick up garbage from the yard.

He was not allowed to play at recess.

KEY WORDS

- indeed
- send (send-sent-sent)
- principal

- be angry with
- have to (= must)
- pick up

- garbage
- be not allowed to + *Verb*
- recess

Sam felt angry.

He also felt hungry.

"What is wrong with you today?" asked his friends.

"You look such a mess.

Your breath smells bad.

You are in a bad mood," said one of them.

- also
- wrong
- such
- mess
- be in a bad mood

Sam felt even more angry. Aha!

He stayed angry all day.

He walked home.

"How was your day?" asked Mom.

"It was a bad day," said Sam.

"But tomorrow will be better."

He smiled to himself.

He had a plan.

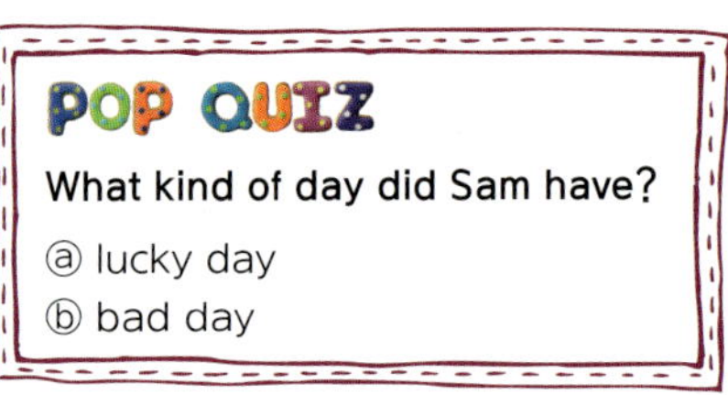

KEY WORDS

- even
- more
- all day
- How was your day?

- bad day
- better
- smile to oneself
- plan

Comprehension Quiz

A   Circle all the words that describe Sam's condition today.

hungry   proud

untidy   mess

scared

B   Put the sentences in order.

❶ Sam walked to school.

❷ Sam woke up late.

❸ Sam came back home.

❹ Sam got into trouble at school.

______ → ______ → ______ → ______

 Choose the best answer to each question.

❶ Why did Sam's mom run after Sam?

a) She wanted to race with him.

b) She wanted to drive him to school.

c) She wanted to give him his bag.

d) She wanted to bring him back home.

❷ What punishment did the principal give to Sam?

a) He had to go home.

b) He had to pick up garbage from the yard at recess.

c) He had to take extra lessons.

d) He had to go to bed early.

❸ After Sam came home, why did he smile while talking with his mom?

a) He had enjoyed his day.

b) He was pleased that people told him what to do.

c) He was glad that it was bedtime.

d) He had a plan for the next day.

Chapter Three

Deep Water

The next day, Sam woke up on time.

He got out of bed.

He ate breakfast.

He brushed his hair.

He brushed his teeth.

He picked up his school bag.

POP QUIZ

What action didn't Sam take this morning?

ⓐ to cook for his mom and dad
ⓑ to brush his teeth

KEY WORDS

- deep
- next day
- do the right thing
- road

Mom smiled.

"You have learned to do the right thing," she said.

"I will drive you to school," said Dad.

"No," said Sam.

"I will walk today."

He walked down the road.

But he did not go to school!

"I am tired of people telling me what to do,"
Sam said.

"I am old enough to do as I please."

Sam's bag was full of heavy books.

He did not want to carry it.

He hid it in a bush.

"I will come back for it later," he said.

Sam did not want to wear his school uniform.

He took off his jacket and hid that in the bush,
too.

KEY WORDS

- be old enough to
- as I please
- be full of
- heavy (↔ light)
- carry
- hide (hide-hid-hidden)
- bush
- come back (come-came-come)
- wear (wear-wore-worn)
- school uniform
- take off
- jacket
- know (know-knew-known)
- schoolboy
- have fun
- about
- hear (hear-heard-heard)
- lake
- swim (swim-swam-swum)
- would like to + *Verb*

"Nobody will know I am a schoolboy," he said.

"I am going to have some fun today."

He thought about what to do.

He had heard that there was a lake in the
forest.

He had heard that people swam in it.

"I would like to go for a swim," he said.

Sam walked to the forest.

There was a sign.

The sign said, "Do Not Enter!"

Sam knew that he should not go in.

The forest looked dark.

Sam was a bit afraid.

But he wanted to go to the lake.

It was a hot day.
Sam thought that
the lake was full
of cool water.
Sam wanted to
swim.
So he went into
the dark forest.
Sam walked
along the path.
The path led to the lake.
The sun was hot.
Sam was hot.

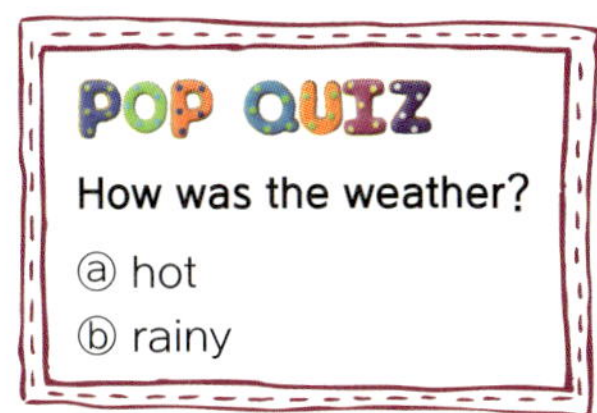

KEY WORDS

- sign
- enter
- should + *Verb*
- dark
- a bit

- afraid
- hot
- cool
- along the path
- lead (lead-led-led)

Finally, he arrived at the lake.

The water looked so cool.

But there was a sign by the lake.

The sign said, "Danger. Deep Water. Do Not Swim."

Sam looked at the sign.

He looked at the lake.

"I want to swim," he said.

He walked past the sign.

He took off most of his clothes.

He jumped into the water.

SPLASH!

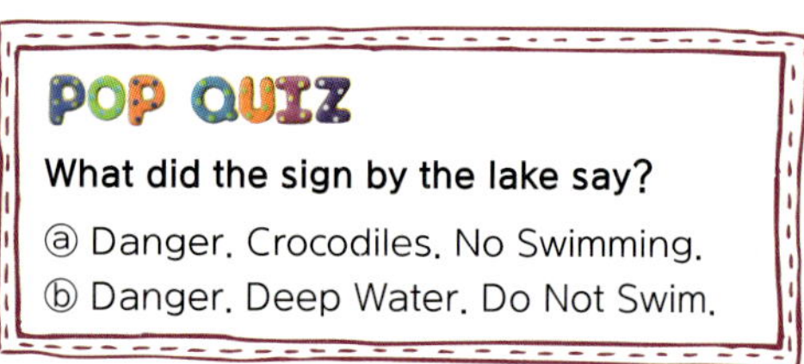

KEY WORDS

- finally
- arrive at
- by
- danger
- past
- most of
- jump into
- splash

SPLASH!
Danger
Deep Water
Do Not Swim

Sam swam in the lake.
The water was cold.
But it was much too cold.
The water was so cold that Sam could not swim. Aha!

His legs did not work properly.
Sam tried to stand up.

But the water was deep.

It was much too deep.

He could not reach the bottom.

"Help!" shouted Sam.

He went under
the water.

He came back
up again,
gasping and
choking.

"Help!" he
shouted again.

"I am going to
drown!"

Comprehension Quiz

A Find the correct word that describes each picture and draw a line connecting them.

❶ 

forest

❷ 

lake

❸ 

Sam's school bag

a) cold

b) dark

c) heavy

B Mark T for true or F for false.

❶ Sam did not take off his clothes to swim. T F

❷ Sam could not reach the bottom of the lake. T F

❸ The weather was very cold. T F

❹ Sam walked into the forest. T F

 Choose the best answer to each question.

❶ Why did Sam say that he would NOT go in Dad's car but would walk to school?

a) He did not like Dad's car.

b) He wanted to arrive at school late.

c) He did not plan to go to school.

d) He liked to exercise a lot.

❷ Why did Sam go into the forest which had a lake?

a) He wanted to hide.

b) He wanted to swim.

c) He wanted to walk.

d) He wanted to sleep.

D Fill in each blank with the right word below.

school	lake	bed	bush

❶ Sam woke up on time and got out of ______________ in the morning.

❷ Dad wanted to drive Sam to ______________.

❸ Sam hid his bag in the ______________.

❹ Finally, Sam arrived at the ______________.

Chapter Four

Happy and Safe

A man ran toward the lake.

A dog ran after him.

The man had a long stick.

"Hold onto the stick!" he called.

"I will pull you out."

Sam reached for the stick.

But his arm did not work properly.

He was too cold.

He went under the water again.

The man jumped into the water.

He swam to Sam.

He put his arms around Sam.

The man lifted Sam up.

He pulled Sam to the edge of the lake.

He pulled Sam out of the water.

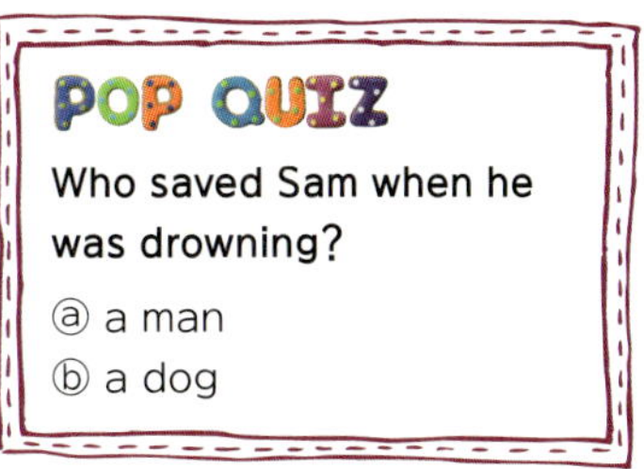

KEY WORDS

- toward
- stick
- hold onto (hold-held-held)
- pull ~ out

- reach for
- put ... around ~
- lift up
- the edge of

Sam lay on the ground.

"Thank you," he gasped.

"Didn't you see the sign?" said the man.

"I own this forest.

I own this lake.

I put the sign there to keep people safe." said the man.

"You are lucky that I was walking my dog.

You could have drowned."

The man took Sam home.

"What happened?" said Mom.

Sam began to cry.

"I am sorry," he said to Mom.

"I did not go to school.

I went to swim in the lake."

"Never do that again!" cried Mom.

"You could have drowned."

Mom thanked the man for saving Sam.

Mom took Sam inside.

He had a hot shower.

"I am sorry," said Sam again.

"I will go to school tomorrow."

"I am sorry too," said Mom.

"You are getting older now. **Aha!**

I will stop telling you what to do all the time.

But now you must think for yourself.

Why do we have rules?

Why do we have signs?

Danger signs are there to keep you safe.

Rules keep everyone safe and happy."

CAUTION
WET
FLOOR

The next morning, Sam woke up on time.

He got out of bed.

He ate breakfast.

He brushed his hair.

He brushed his teeth.

He went to pick up his school bag.

"Oh no!" he said.
"My school bag is in
a bush.
My jacket is there
too!"
Dad smiled.
"We can pick them up on
the way to school.
Will you let me drive you
today?"
"Yes," said Sam.
"Thank you."

POP QUIZ

Where are Sam's bag and uniform jacket?

ⓐ in his room
ⓑ in a bush

KEY WORDS

▪ on the way to school

▪ **let** (let-let-let)

Sam went to school.

His friends were pleased to see him. 

He was not angry.

He was not hungry.

He was not afraid.

He was not in danger.

Instead, he had another feeling.

"I feel happy," he said.

"I feel safe."

KEY WORDS

- be pleased to + *Verb*
- be in danger
- instead
- another
- feeling

A Who said what? Match each line with the right person.

❶ 

a) "Rules keep everyone safe and happy."

❷ 

b) "You are lucky that I was walking my dog."

❸ 

c) "I feel happy."

B Mark T for true or F for false.

❶ Sam woke up on time this morning.   T   F

❷ Mom brushed Sam's hair.   T   F

❸ Sam did not eat breakfast this morning.   T   F

❹ Dad was angry that Sam did not have his bag.   T   F

 Fill in each blank with the right word below.

friends	drive	sign	lake

❶ The man jumped into the ______________ to save Sam.

❷ The ______________ was there to keep people safe.

❸ Sam let his dad ______________ him to school.

❹ Sam's ______________ were pleased to see him.

D Put the sentences in order.

❶ The man pulled Sam out of the water.

❷ The man held out a long stick to Sam.

❸ The man put his arms around Sam.

❹ The man jumped into the water.

______ → ______ → ______ → ______

Let's Review the Story

Fill in the blanks to review the story.

Title: Do As I Tell You!

Chapter One:

- Sam's ____________, dad and ____________ kept telling him what to do.
- Sam did not like it, but he did what they told him.

Chapter Two:

- Sam did not do the things he was told to do.
- He was ____________ for school and he got into t ____________ .
- He was also h ____________ and angry.

Chapter Three:

- Sam did not go to ____________ .
- Instead, he went to a lake in the ____________ .
- Sam swam in the lake, but it was cold and ____________ .
- He almost drowned.

Chapter Four:

- Sam was rescued by a ____________ .
- Mom told Sam that he had to think of rules and danger signs for himself.
- He felt happy and ____________ in the school.

Let's Think & Talk

Think about the following questions and answer them freely.

❶ Do you have things that you don't want to do but your parents or teachers make you do them? Why do your parents or teachers get you to do such things? Share your thoughts.

❷ In some cases, rules can be very annoying and sometimes you don't want to keep them. In spite of that, why do rules exist? Tell us your opinion.

❸ What danger signs have you seen recently? Why were they put up and what safety accident do they prevent?

Let's Review the Story

Title: Do As I Tell You!

Chapter One:

- Sam's **mom**, dad and **teacher(s)** kept telling him what to do.
- Sam did not like it, but he did what they told him.

Chapter Two:

- Sam did not do the things he was told to do.
- He was **late** for school and he got into **trouble**.
- He was also **hungry** and angry.

Chapter Three:

- Sam did not go to **school**.
- Instead, he went to a lake in the **forest**.
- Sam swam in the lake, but it was cold and **deep**.
- He almost drowned.

Chapter Four:

- Sam was rescued by a **man**.
- Mom told Sam that he had to think of rules and danger signs for himself.
- He felt happy and **safe** in the school.

Smart Readers: **Wise** & **Wide**

After-reading Test

- Do As I Tell You!
- Level 1
- 19 Questions

  (Vocabulary 5 / Reading Comprehension 10 /

  Sentence Structure & Grammar 4)

1. Which of the following does NOT have the same meaning as the rest?
   ① get dressed   ② put on
   ③ take off   ④ pull on

2. Which of the following is NOT a word that describes a feeling?
   ① angry
   ② afraid
   ③ happy
   ④ hurry

3. Which is NOT a pair of words that are opposites?
   ① safe ↔ dangerous
   ② hot ↔ cool
   ③ happy ↔ lucky
   ④ empty ↔ full

4. Which pair has the wrong past tense form of the listed verb?
   ① begin – began
   ② tell – told
   ③ put – putted
   ④ feel – felt

5. Choose the right word for the blank.

   > You can get to school ____________ time.

   ① by   ② on
   ③ to   ④ for

6. Choose all the reasons why the teacher was angry at Sam.
① Sam was late for school.
② Sam did badly on the quiz.
③ Sam did not bring his books.
④ Sam was rude to the teacher.

7. Why did Sam want to do as he pleased?
① He thought he was old enough.
② He thought he was wise enough.
③ He thought he was strong enough.
④ He thought he was tall enough.

8. Which one is NOT a thing that Sam has to do every morning?
① to brush his hair
② to brush his teeth
③ to eat breakfast
④ to go to dark forest

9. What did NOT happen to Sam on the day when he was late for school?
① He was sent to the principal.
② He was not allowed to play at recess.
③ He had to pick up garbage.
④ He did the quiz very well.

10. What did the sign by the lake NOT say?
① Danger.
② Cold Water.
③ Do Not Swim.
④ Deep Water.

11. Why did Sam feel afraid when he arrived at the forest?
① The weather was getting colder.
② He did not like being alone.
③ He saw that the forest looked dark.
④ He did not know the way home.

12. Why could Sam NOT move his legs freely in the water?
① He hit against a rock.
② He was sick.
③ He was very tired.
④ He was too cold.

13. Which of the following is NOT right about the man who saved Sam?
① He owned the forest.
② He jumped into the water.
③ He was walking his dog.
④ He took Sam to hospital.

14. What did Sam's mom do to the man who saved Sam?
① She thanked the man.
② She gave the man a gift.
③ She said sorry to the man.
④ She invited the man to stay for a meal.

15. Why did Sam's mom say that Sam should follow rules and danger signs?
① Rules and danger signs keep everyone safe and happy.
② Rules and danger signs make people dangerous.
③ Rules and danger signs are important only for students.
④ Rules and danger signs were made by adults.

16.

"You must to get up," said Mom.
  ① ②   ③   ④

17.

Sam felt even more angrily.
  ① ② ③   ④

18.

The water was so cold this Sam could not swim.
     ① ② ③   ④

19. Choose the correct word or phrase for the blank.

"I will ___________ you to school."

① drive   ② to drive
③ driving   ④ be driven

Memo

Memo

Memo 

Memo

Sarah J. Dodd
Sarah J. Dodd is an experienced primary school teacher who resides in the UK, but has also lived and taught in Australia. She has a PhD in Science and a certificate in Creative Writing. She has published several books for children: "An Angel Anyway" (Anyway Press, 2008) the "Little Angels" series (Lion Children's Books, 2009/10), "The Lion Picture Bible" (Lion Children's Books, 2015) and "Legs: the tale of a meerkat lost and found" (Lion Children's Books, 2015). Her poetry for children has also been highly commended and published in the anthology "Let in the Stars" (Manchester Metropolitan University, 2014).
She is currently working on further picture books for the very young, and a novel for older children.

Do As I Tell You!

Written by Sarah J. Dodd
Illustrated by Hyeseon Ahn

First published August 2015
2nd printing July 2022

Publisher: Kyudo Chung
Editors: Juyon Choi, Jiyeong Park, Kyunghee Jang
Designers: Eunhee Lee, Elim

Published and distributed by
Happy House, an Imprint of DARAKWON, Inc.
Darakwon Bldg., 211 Munbal-ro, Paju-si, Gyeonggi-do, 10881, Republic of Korea
Tel: 82-2-736-2031(ext. 250)   Fax: 82-2-732-2037
Homepage: www.ihappyhouse.co.kr

ISBN: 978-89-6653-199-8 18740 / 978-89-6653-156-1 18740(set)

[Components]
• 1 Audio CD (Recording Studio: Aram)
• Answer Keys & Korean Translation: Free download at www.ihappyhouse.co.kr